THE HIPPO CHRISTMAS JOKE BOOK

"What did Santa get when he crossed a reindeer with a plank of wood?
A hat rack.

How do sheep keep warm at the North Pole?
Central bleating.

What is Mrs Santa's real name?
Mary Christmas."

Santa and his friends invite you to join them and enjoy their jokey fun-filled Christmas!
And a Very Hippo Christmas to you!!

THE HIPPO CHRISTMAS JOKE BOOK

compiled by Chris Muskard
illustrated by Stuart Trotter

Hippo Books
Scholastic Publications Limited
London

Scholastic Publications Ltd.,
10 Earlham Street, London WC2H 9RX, UK

Scholastic Inc.,
730 Broadway, New York, NY 10003, USA

Scholastic Tab Publications Ltd.,
123 Newkirk Road, Richmond Hill,
Ontario L4C 3G5, Canada

Ashton Scholastic Pty. Ltd.,
PO Box 579, Gosford, New South Wales,
Australia

Ashton Scholastic Ltd.,
165 Marua Road, Panmure, Auckland 6,
New Zealand

First published by Scholastic Publications Limited, UK, 1987

Text copyright © Victorama Limited, 1987
Illustrations © Stuart Trotter, 1987

ISBN 0 590 70808 2

Made and printed by Cox and Wyman, Reading, Berks
Typeset in Plantin by AKM Associates (UK) Ltd.,
Ajmal House, Hayes Road, Southall, London

A LETTER FROM SANTA

Christmas Cottage,
The Toy Factory,
North Pole

Hello,

Every year thousands of boys and girls write to me to ask about my life at the North Pole — so this year I and my friends have decided to write to you! We have a wonderful time here at the North Pole, and while we're making toys and gifts in our Toy Factory we tell each other jokes. The Hippo Christmas Joke Book *is a collection of our favourite funny stories and riddles and we're sure that you'll enjoy them too! Let me introduce you to all my friends.*

You've probably heard of **Rudolph the Red-Nosed Reindeer**. *Each Christmas Eve Rudolph and his team pull my sleigh through the sky so that I can deliver everyone's presents. Have you ever seen us?*

Lots of people ask me how I manage to deliver so many presents in just one night. The answer is that I have help! **Nosey the Gnome** *rides with me on my sleigh and drops presents down the chimneys we fly over each Christmas. He also keeps the reindeer quiet so that we don't wake anyone up, but if you listen carefully on Christmas Eve you'll be able to hear the bells on Rudolph's harness jingling as we fly!*

Back at the Toy Factory I have two Elf helpers, **Stripe** *and* **Flash**. *Stripe makes all the toys and presents that children receive on Christmas Eve, and he wraps them carefully in sparkly Christmas paper. Flash takes charge of all the letters that children send me. He makes lists of the gifts that everyone asks for so that I*

5

deliver the right things on Christmas Eve. Sometimes he gets a bit muddled up — so if you got a dozen pairs of woolly socks last year, instead of the BMX bike or the computer you asked for, Flash sends his apologies. He'll try to get it right this year!

Fairy Silver lives at the North Pole with us too. She is in charge of all the Christmas fairies who decorate the tops of Christmas trees. If you don't have a fairy for the top of your Christmas tree, why not write to Fairy Silver and ask her to send one?

Last of all there is my wife, **Mrs Santa**, who looks after everyone here at the North Pole — including **Snowball** our pet baby polar bear. When he grows up Snowball will help us in the Toy Factory, but at the moment he prefers to play with the toys instead!

We all hope you enjoy our jokes — and Merry Christmas from all of us here at the North Pole!

With love from
Santa
(and Snowball)

SANTA'S CHRISTMAS CHUCKLE

What nationality is Santa?
North Polish!

Nosey the Gnome was asking Santa lots of silly questions. "I can't stop and answer them now," grumbled Santa. "Remember, curiosity killed the cat, Nosey."

"Really?" asked Nosey. "What did the cat want to know?"

Santa and Flash the Elf went to a restaurant for lunch.

"Waiter, waiter," Flash called, "there's a spider in my butter!"

"It's impossible," protested the waiter. "We only use margarine in this restaurant."

RUDOLPH THE REINDEER'S RIDDLE

What does Rudolph say before he tells a joke?
This one will sleigh you!

What is the difference between teachers and Christmas presents?
Children love Christmas presents.

Stripe went to see the doctor because he had some big spots on his face. "Doctor, doctor," he asked, "can you make my spots go away?"

"Well," said the doctor, "I can't make any rash promises."

What do jelly babies wear on their feet?
Gum boots.

What is a duck's favourite television programme?
The Feather Forecast.

What is the name for a musical insect?
A humbug.

Why did Robin Hood only steal from rich people?
Because poor people didn't have anything worth taking.

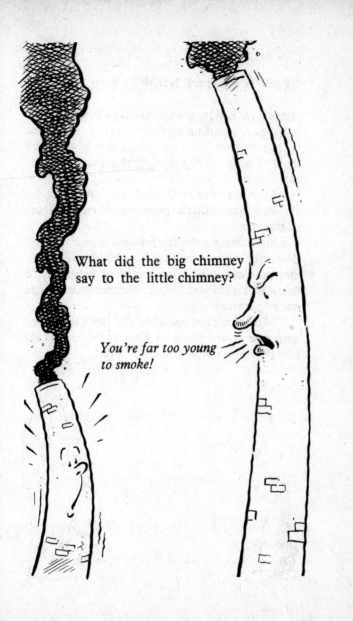

What did the big chimney say to the little chimney?

You're far too young to smoke!

STRIPE'S SILLY STORY

A man was out for a walk one day when he found a penguin standing on the pavement. It looked so lonely that he could not leave it there by itself. "What shall I do with this penguin?" he asked a policeman who was passing by.

"Take it to the zoo," said the policeman. So the man picked up the penguin and carried it off to the zoo.

Later the same day the policeman was walking down the street when he saw the man again — and he was still carrying the penguin. "I thought I told you to take the penguin to the zoo?" he asked.

"I did," said the man. "We've been to the zoo and now we're going to have some ice-cream before we go to the cinema."

FAIRY SILVER'S FAVOURITE JOKE
What do Santa's Elves like to eat for tea?
Fairy cakes.

Knock, knock.
Who's there?
Boo.
Boo who?
Oh, please don't cry!

What pudding is yellow and bad-tempered?
Apple grumble.

What does Luke Skywalker shave with?
A laser blade.

STRIPE: What has ten hairy brown legs, three red eyes and is covered in purple fur?
FAIRY SILVER: I don't know.
STRIPE: Neither do I, but there's one creeping up the back of your neck!

11

FLASH'S FUNNY HA-HA

FLASH: Why don't you do any more tap-dancing?
NOSEY: I had to give it up.
FLASH: Why?
NOSEY: I kept falling into the sink!

Where should you take a sick wasp?
To the waspital.

What do you call a rabbit with fleas?
Bugs Bunny.

What is always coming but never actually arrives?
Tomorrow, because by the time it arrives it's today.

MRS SANTA'S CHRISTMAS GIGGLE

What is Mrs Santa's real name?
Mary Christmas!

Knock, knock,
Who's there?
Felix.
Felix who?
Felix my ice cream once more I'll scream!

What is the difference between an elephant and a biscuit?
You can't dip an elephant in your milk.

Flash the Elf made dinner for everyone last week, but he's not a very good cook.

"What is it, Flash?" asked Mrs Santa when he served the meal.

"It's cottage pie," said Flash.

Mrs Santa ate a mouthful. "Yes, I can tell," she said. "I think I've just found a brick."

What has a bottom at its top?
A leg.

What's the best way to keep Britain tidy?
Send all the rubbish to America.

What is a frog's favourite sweet?
A lollihop.

What cars do hot dogs like driving?
A Rolls.

Why do cats have fur coats?
*Because they would look silly
in plastic macs.*

What breakfast cereal do ghosts like to eat?
Dreaded Wheat.

NOSEY'S CRAZY QUESTIONS

What happened when Popeye tried to make a pizza?
There was Olive Oyl all over the place!

What's yellow, brown and hairy?
Cheese on toast dropped on the carpet.

What do you get if you cross a polar bear with a kangaroo?
A fur coat with enormous pockets.

What do you call a reindeer with one eye?
I've no idea.

Why do giraffes have such long necks?
Because their feet smell terrible.

Knock, knock.
Who's there?
Police.
Police who?
Police to meet you.

Who held the baby octopus hostage?
Squidnappers.

SANTA'S CHRISTMAS CHUCKLE

Who won the Monster Beauty Contest?
No one.

What flavour crisps are named after a desert ruler?
Sultan Vinegar.

What kind of exams did Santa pass?
Ho-ho-ho levels.

STRIPE: What is the connection between a banana, a lemon and a pot of glue?
FLASH: A banana and a lemon are both yellow fruit, but I don't know about the pot of glue.
STRIPE: I knew you'd get stuck with it.

MRS SANTA: Eat your cabbage, Santa. It will put some colour in your cheeks.
SANTA: But I don't want green cheeks.

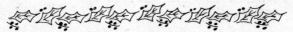

RUDOLPH THE REINDEER'S RIDDLE

What is the wettest sort of animal?
A reindeer.

NOSEY: I'm going to prove that you're not here.
STRIPE: How are you going to do that?
NOSEY: Tell me, are you in New York?
STRIPE: No.
NOSEY: Are you in Rome?
STRIPE: No.
NOSEY: Are you in London?
STRIPE: No.
NOSEY: Well, if you're not in New York and you're not in Rome and you're not in London, you must be somewhere else. And if you're somewhere else you're not here!

What has 2000 eyes and 2000 legs?
1000 people.

What sort of fish makes a nice pudding?
Jellyfish.

Why do bank managers carry briefcases?
Because briefcases can't walk.

There were three cats in a boat. One jumped out and fell into the water. How many cats were left in the boat?
None, because they were copycats.

What is always behind time?
The back of a clock.

What do policemen like in their sandwiches?
Pork truncheon meat.

Why was the robot so silly?
Because he had a screw loose.

Knock, knock.
Who's there?
Luke.
Luke who?
Luke through the keyhole and you'll see!

FLASH'S FUNNY HA-HA

Did you hear about the man who was arrested for doing his Christmas shopping early?
He was caught in Marks and Spencers at three o'clock in the morning!

Why can't two elephants go swimming at the same time?
Because they only have one pair of trunks.

Flash went out to play with his sledge in the snow, and before long Stripe joined him. "Can I share your sledge?" he asked.

"O.K.," said Flash.

"That's great!" said Stripe.

Flash handed him the sledge. "You can have it going uphill, I'll have it going downhill."

Which TV show do cleaning ladies like best?
"The Moppets."

MRS SANTA'S CHRISTMAS GIGGLE

MRS SANTA: Why is our Christmas pudding like the sea?
SANTA: I don't know!
MRS SANTA: Because it's full of currants.

Knock, knock.
Who's there?
Godfrey.
Godfrey who?
Godfrey tickets for the pictures!

Which box can never keep a secret?
A chatterbox.

Which are the fastest type of beans?
Runner beans.

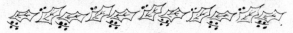

SNOWBALL'S SNIGGERS

NOSEY: I wonder where fleas go in winter?
SNOWBALL: Search me!

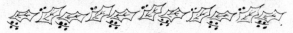

Where does Tarzan buy his clothes?
At the jungle sale.

Stripe was helping Nosey to load Christmas presents onto Santa's sleigh. "Did you know that the most brilliant person in the world was going deaf?" he asked.

"No, I didn't. Who is he?" said Nosey.

"Pardon?" said Stripe.

What do you call a man with meat, potatoes and gravy on his head?
Stew.

What is Christmas called in Great Britain?
Yule Britannia.

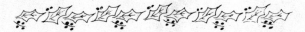

NOSEY'S CRAZY QUESTIONS

What does the Queen do when Prince Harry burps?
She issues a Royal Pardon.

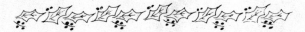

STRIPE: I used to snore very loudly. Sometimes I used to wake myself up.
FLASH: Have you cured the problem?
STRIPE: Yes, now I sleep in a different room.

What is a hedgehog's favourite food?
Prickled onions.

An old lady was making her first flight in an aeroplane and she was very nervous. "What happens if we run out of fuel?" she asked the pilot when she got on board.

"We all get out and push," he said.

SANTA'S CHRISTMAS CHUCKLE

Why does Santa always climb down chimneys?
Because it soots him!

NOSEY: Did you know that it takes three sheep to make one jumper?
RUDOLPH: I didn't even know that sheep could knit!

What did the vegetables say when they knocked on the door?
Lettuce in!

The three bears came downstairs for breakfast. "Who's been eating *my* porridge?" asked Father Bear, looking at his empty bowl.

"Who's been eating *my* porridge?" asked Baby Bear, looking at *his* empty bowl.

"Be quiet, both of you," said Mother Bear. "I haven't had time to make it yet."

What musical instruments do mice play?
Mouse organs.

"Doctor, doctor," complained a patient, "I feel like a goat."

"How long have you felt like this?" asked the doctor.

"Since I was a kid."

RUDOLPH THE REINDEER'S RIDDLE

Why do reindeer have wrinkled knees?
Have you ever tried to iron a reindeer?

How can you tell one kind of cat from another?
Look it up in a catalogue.

Why did the golfer wear an extra pair of trousers?
In case he got a hole in one.

What is white and flies upwards?
A stupid snowflake.

What is a thief's favourite food?
Hamburglars.

FLASH'S FUNNY HA-HA

What should you feed undernourished elves?
Elf-raising flour.

STRIPE: I was going to buy you a handker-chief for Christmas.
NOSEY: That was very kind — but why didn't you give me one?
STRIPE: I couldn't find one big enough!

"Waiter, waiter," protested Santa, "there's a button in my salad."

"It must have fallen off your jacket potato, sir."

What do you get if you cross a kilt and a frog?
Hopscotch.

"Doctor, doctor, I keep thinking I'm a dog."

"Hop up onto the couch and I'll examine you."

"I'm not allowed on the furniture!"

What did the hamburger say to the tomato?
I've had enough of your sauce!

Who helps sick fairies and elves?
The National Elf Service.

What do you get if you cross a snowman with a shark?
Frostbite.

What do you call a boy with a spade on his head?
Doug.

NEWSFLASH: A lorry carrying sugar has collided with a van carrying candy floss on the M1 motorway. Police are advising drivers to stick to their lanes.

What should you call the story of the three little pigs?
A pigtail.

What do short-sighted ghosts wear?
Spooktacles.

Knock, knock.
Who's there?
Ivor.
Ivor who?
Ivor terrible headache.

MRS SANTA'S CHRISTMAS GIGGLE

What happened when Mrs Santa crossed a turkey with an octopus?
Everyone had a leg for Christmas dinner.

Why is it difficult to keep a secret at the North Pole?
Because your teeth chatter.

STRIPE: Why do elephants paint their toe-nails orange?

NOSEY: I don't know.

STRIPE: So that they can hide upside down in pots of marmalade.

NOSEY: I don't believe that!

STRIPE: Have you ever seen an elephant in your marmalade?

NOSEY: No.

STRIPE: That just proves how well it works!

What's black and white and red all over?
A penguin with sunburn.

SNOWBALL'S SNIGGER

What's white, furry and smells of peppermint?
A Polo bear!

What do you call a penguin in the desert?
Lost.

"Doctor, doctor, I keep seeing double!"
   "Lie down on the couch."
   "Which one?"

Did you hear that two burglars have escaped from prison? One is one metre eighty, the other is just under a metre. The police are looking high and low for them.

What is the crocodile's favourite card game?
Snap.

What do you give a sick budgie?
Tweetment.

NOSEY'S CRAZY QUESTION

What should you do if your nose goes on strike?
Pick it.

SANTA: Snowball is just like one of the family!
MRS SANTA: Which one of us?

What never asks questions but gets plenty of answers?
A doorbell.

What did the Scout master say when he'd had his car horn fixed?
Beep repaired.

"Doctor, doctor, I've swallowed a pen! What shall I do?"
   "Use a pencil until I get there."

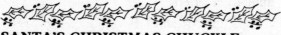

SANTA'S CHRISTMAS CHUCKLE

What did Santa buy the deaf fish for Christmas?
A herring aid.

A large family went out for the day to the safari park. They drove round the lions' enclosure in their car.
   "It's so cruel," said one of the lions. "Look at them all caged up like that!"

Should you say "Six and nine *is* fourteen" or "six and nine *are* fourteen?"
Neither – six and nine are fifteen!

What has a neck but can't swallow?
A bottle.

What do frogs sit on?
Toadstools.

What begins with P, ends with E, and has millions of letters?
The Post Office.

Two space creatures from the planet Mars landed in a deserted street late one night. There was nothing around except for a set of traffic lights. "I love you," said one Martian, going down on his knees. "Will you marry me?"

"Get up," said the other. "I was the one she winked at."

What do you get if you cross a parrot and a centipede?
A walkie-talkie.

Who designed the world's first rainjacket?
Anna Rack.

What is yellow outside, grey inside and has a good memory?
An elephant omelette.

Why did the bun taste like soap?
Because it was a bath bun.

STRIPE'S SILLY STORY

Three boys went into a sweet shop. "I'd like twenty pence worth of toffee — the toffee in the jar on the top shelf," said one boy. The sweet shop owner climbed onto a chair, took down the jar of toffees, weighed out twenty pence worth and then climbed up on the chair to replace the jar.

"I'd like twenty pence worth of that toffee on the top shelf too, please," said the second boy. With a sigh, the sweet shop owner climbed back up onto the chair, took down the jar and weighed out another twenty pence worth of toffee.

"I suppose that *you* want twenty pence worth of this toffee too," he said to the third boy.

"No, thanks," said the boy. So the sweet shop owner climbed back on the chair and put the jar back in its place. When he got back down he turned to the third boy.

"What *would* you like?"

"I'd like *thirty* pence worth of that toffee on the top shelf, please."

Why do fast cars suffer from aches and pains?
They have vroomatism.

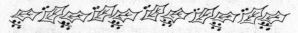

FAIRY SILVER'S FAVOURITE JOKE

Which sort of elf eats its food quickly?
A goblin.

STRIPE: Would you like a pocket calculator for Christmas?
NOSEY: No thank you.
STRIPE: Why not?
NOSEY: Because I already know how many pockets I've got.

Two snakes were sitting on a rock. "Ouch!" said one. "Are we poisonous snakes?"

"No, I don't think so," said the other.

"That's good," said the first. "I've just bitten my lip."

What did one lift say to the other lift?
I think I'm going down with something.

What do you call a man in a barrel in the sea?
Bob.

FLASH'S FUNNY HA-HA

What did one Christmas cracker say to the other Christmas cracker?
I bet my pop's bigger than your pop!

What often falls at the North Pole but never gets hurt?
Snow.

What do you call a foreign body in a chip pan?
An Unidentified Frying Object.

Why do bees fly through the air with their back legs crossed?
They're looking for a BP station.

A motorist pulled into the kerb to ask directions. "What's the best way to Bath?" he asked a lady.
   "You need soap, a towel and plenty of hot water . . . ."

A boy crawled into the classroom on his hands and knees when the lesson was already under way. "Why are you crawling into class, Richard?" asked his teacher.
   "You told me never to walk in late, so I'm not!"

What do parking wardens eat for lunch?
Traffic jam sandwiches.

What do you get if you cross a rabbit and a bunch of leeks?
Bunions.

Why aren't they growing bananas any longer?
Because bananas are long enough already.

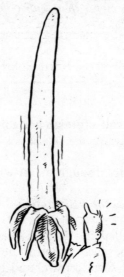

Knock, knock.
Who's there?
Snow.
Snow who?
Snow good asking me, *I* don't know.

If a blue house is made of blue bricks and a red house is made of red bricks, what is a green-house made of?
Glass.

What did the composer write in the bath?
Soap operas.

What do you get if you cross a zebra and a pig?
Striped sausages.

SNOWBALL'S SNIGGERS
What should you call a bald teddy?
Fred bear.

A young girl was talking to her teacher. "I don't think my mother likes me very much," she said.

"Why do you think that?" asked the teacher.

"Every day when she makes my sandwiches for lunch, she wraps them in a road map."

"Doctor, doctor, people think I'm lying all the time."

"I can't believe it."

Why did the tiger cross the road?
Because it was the chicken's day off.

Did you hear what happened to the girl who was sawed in half by a magician?
She's living in London and Manchester.

A posh lady was sitting on a train next to a boy who kept sniffing. After a few minutes she turned to the boy and said, "Don't you have a handkerchief?"

"Yes," he replied, "but I'm not allowed to lend it to strangers."

Why did the manager of the bath sponge factory
refuse to resign?
Because he found the job too absorbing.

STRIPE'S SILLY STORY

A boastful American man went to stay with his
Australian cousin. The cousin took him out for
trips to see the country. On their first outing
they saw the Sydney Opera House. "What do
you think?" the Australian asked proudly.

"Very nice — but back in America we have
dog kennels bigger than that," said the American. On their next trip they went to see the
enormous desert.

"It's impressive," said the American, "but
back home my garden is bigger than this." His
Australian cousin was beginning to feel very fed
up. Then suddenly a kangaroo bounced past.

"Wow!" said the American. "I'll say this for
Australia — your fleas are bigger than American
ones!"

Why did the blind chicken cross the road?
To get to the Birds Eye shop.

FLASH: I'm not myself tonight.
STRIPE: I noticed the improvement.

What do you call a school jacket on fire?
A blazer.

What do you call a man with
a car on his head?
Jack.

Why is Prince Charles like a cloudy day?
Because he will reign.

STRIPE: I used to be twins.
FLASH: How do you know?
STRIPE: My mum has a picture of me when I
was two.

FAIRY SILVER'S FAVOURITE JOKE

Why can only tiny fairies sit under toadstools?
Because there isn't mushroom.

Why does an elephant have cracks between his toes?
To hold his bus ticket.

Where was Magna Carta signed?
At the bottom.

"Waiter, waiter, there's a spider playing football in my saucer!"
   "Yes, sir, and tomorrow he'll be playing in the cup."

Where do you take sick ponies?
To the horsepital.

FLASH'S FUNNY HA-HA

Knock, knock.
Who's there?
Thumping.
Thumping who?
Thumping nice in my Chrithmath thtocking pleathe, Thanta!

Where do cows go when they want an evening out?
The moooo-vies.

What do you call a judge with no fingers?
Justice Thumbs.

In which country are there no fat people?
Finland.

MRS SANTA'S CHRISTMAS GIGGLE

What do you call a tug-of-war on 24 December?
Christmas Heave.

What happened when the two kangaroos got married?
They lived hoppily ever after.

NOSEY: I think Stripe must have been put together upside down.
FLASH: Why?
NOSEY: Because his nose runs and his feet smell.

What happened when the lion ate Jasper Carrott?
He felt funny.

How can you tell when a train has gone?
It leaves tracks behind.

"Doctor, doctor, I've only got fifty-nine seconds to live!"
    "Sit down for a minute . . . ."

How can you spell hungry horse in four letters?
M T G G.

Why did the hamburger blush?
It saw the salad dressing.

SNOWBALL'S SNIGGERS

What is the best way to hunt bear?
Take all your clothes off first!

What do you call a ghostly doctor?
A surgical spirit.

NOSEY'S CRAZY QUESTIONS

What is the difference between a nail and a bad boxer?
One is knocked in and the other is knocked out.

Which bus sailed the ocean to America?
Christopher Columbus.

What would you get if you crossed a sheep with a shower of rain?
A wet blanket.

Did you hear about the boxing chicken?
He was the featherweight champion.

What happened to the stupid jellyfish?
It set.

NOSEY: Do you have holes in your socks?
SANTA: No I don't!
NOSEY: Then how do you get your feet in them?

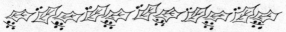

SANTA'S CHRISTMAS CHUCKLE

How does Santa dress at the North Pole?
Quickly!

Where does Superman buy all the food he needs to keep him big and strong?
At the supermarket.

RUDOLPH THE REINDEER'S RIDDLE

Did you hear the story of the three reindeer?
No? Oh dear, dear, dear.

What do you call two chemists' shops side by side?
A pair of Boots.

What kind of cups can't you drink from?
Buttercups and hiccups.

STRIPE: What an amazing pair of socks, Santa. One has red and white spots, the other has green and blue stripes.
SANTA: Yes — and I've got another pair just like them at home!

What's the biggest mouse in the world?
A hippopotamouse.

What gets wetter the more it dries?
A towel.

STRIPE: I've just brought a parrot that can count.

NOSEY: Really?

STRIPE: Watch. What's nought plus nought, Polly?

NOSEY: He's not saying anything.

STRIPE: That's because the answer is nothing.

What happened when Mrs Santa served soap-flakes instead of cornflakes for breakfast?
Santa was so angry he foamed at the mouth.

A boy came home from his first day at his new school. "My teacher really likes me," said the boy.

"That's good," said his dad. "How do you know she likes you?"

"She keeps putting little crosses in my exercise book."

"Doctor, doctor, I've just swallowed a spoon!"

"Sit still and don't stir."

FAIRY SILVER'S FAVOURITE JOKE

What is Fairy Silver's favourite book?
The Fairy On The Christmas Tree by Holly Branch and Miss L. Toe.

Why do witches ride broomsticks?
Because their vacuum cleaner leads are too short.

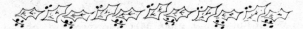

FLASH'S FUNNY HA-HA

What is the best day to eat fish and chips?
Fry-day.

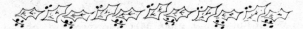

What did the burglar say when he stole a man's watch?
I'm sorry to have taken your time.

What happened to the man who invented electricity?
He got a terrible shock.

How do monsters count to twenty-one?
On their fingers.

The children were being very noisy in class.
  "Order, children, order!" cried the teacher.
  One cheeky boy called out, "A hamburger and chips for me please, Miss!"

Why are bananas never lonely?
Because they always hang around in bunches.

What happened when Stripe was locked out of the Toy Factory?
He sang a tune until he found the right key.

What is lighter than a feather but impossible to hold for long?
Your breath.

Which bird is always out of breath?
A puffin.

SNOWBALL'S SNIGGERS

STRIPE: Snowball is a very cheap pet to feed.
NOSEY: Why is that?
STRIPE: Because he's a polar bear and polar bears live on ice.

Knock, knock.
Who's there?
Julie.
Julie who?
Julie eve any dinner for me?

What kind of vegetables do plumbers like best?
Leeks.

How do you make a baby sleep in space?
Rock-et.

What happens if you cross a skunk with a boomerang?
You get a nasty smell that always comes back.

Why do tigers
eat raw meat?
*Because no one
taught them to cook.*

Which burn longer, the candles on a boy's birthday cake or the candles on a girl's birthday cake?
Neither – all candles burn shorter.

Why are the songs sung in church called hymns and not hers?
Because they finish Amen and not Awomen.

What do we call the man who owns all the cows
in Saudi Arabia?
A milk sheikh.

SANTA'S CHRISTMAS CHUCKLE

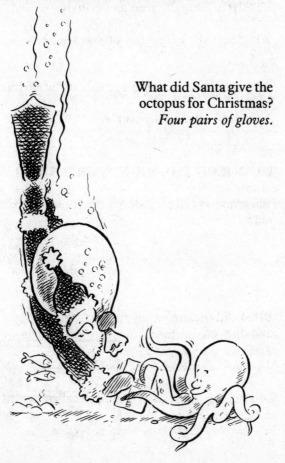

What did Santa give the
octopus for Christmas?
Four pairs of gloves.

What is a vampire's favourite sport?
Batminton.

STRIPE: You've got a face like a million dollars.
NOSEY: Have I really?
STRIPE: Yes, all green and crinkly.

Who leads the ladies' tug-of-war team?
Eve.

Why should you never play cards in the African bush?
Because of all the cheetahs there.

RUDOLPH THE REINDEER'S RIDDLE

What do you call a reindeer with a number on its tail?
Reg.

What did the carpet say to the dresser?
I can see your drawers!

FAIRY SILVER'S FAVOURITE JOKE

What wobbles as it flies?
A jellycopter.

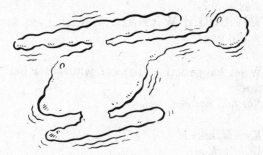

What happened when Fairy Silver ate a Christmas tree decoration?
She caught tinselitis.

SANTA: Are you chewing gum?
STRIPE: No, I'm Stripe the Elf!

Why don't they eat custard in China?
Have you ever tried eating custard with chopsticks?

What do you call a pony with a sore throat?
A hoarse horse.

Did you hear about the stupid ghost?
He climbed over walls!

What do Eskimos call their cash?
Ice lolly.

Why did the policeman wear orange braces?
To keep his trousers up.

INVISIBLE MAN: Did you miss me while I was gone?
INVISIBLE WOMAN: I didn't even know you'd gone!

What happened to the cat who ate a ball of wool?
She had mittens.

Knock, knock.
Who's there?
Watson.
Watson who?
Watson television tonight?

What's red and cheeky?
Tomato sauce.

Why do dustmen always say no?
Because they are refuse men.

FLASH'S FUNNY HA-HA

What does Nosey say when he gets back to the North Pole after delivering the presents on Christmas Eve?
Gnome, sweet gnome.

What kind of feet do maths teachers have?
Square feet.

"Waiter, waiter, there's a twig in my soup."
"I know, sir. We have branches everywhere."

What kind of food do Italian spooks like most?
Spooketti.

Where do snowmen go dancing?
At the snowball.

MRS SANTA'S CHRISTMAS GIGGLE

Why does Mrs Santa wear curlers in bed on Christmas Eve?
Because she wants to wake up curly in the morning.

What goes tick-tick-woof-woof?
A watchdog.

What's the best way to make time fly?
Throw a clock over your shoulder.

Can a match box?
No, but a tin can.

What did one polite sheep say to the other at the gate?
After ewe.

Why are wolves like playing cards?
Because they both come in packs.

SNOWBALL'S SNIGGERS

Which bear got off the train at the wrong London station and never became famous?
Waterloo bear.

What do disc jockeys wear?
Track suits.

Have you heard about the latest burglarproof houses?
They are built by Surelock Homes.

Why are kangaroos waiting eagerly for 1988?
Because it's a leap year.

SANTA'S CHRISTMAS CHUCKLE

SANTA: The doctor's put me on a seafood diet.
NOSEY: Has he really?
SANTA: Yes, if I see food I eat it.

What is the quickest way to get to the bus stop?
Run like mad.

SANTA: Why are you jumping up and down?
NOSEY: I've just taken some medicine but I forgot to shake the bottle.

What did the robber say when he broke into the glue factory?
"This is a stick-up!"

What is short and green and helps old ladies across the road?
A Brussels scout.

What is brown on the outside, grey on the inside and a meal in itself?
A wholemeal elephant sandwich.

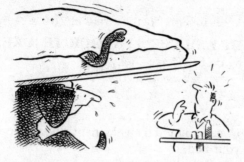

What kind of ant is good at adding up?
An accountant.

FLASH: I can move so much faster when I have a cold.
STRIPE: That's strange.
FLASH: No it's not — it's because I've got a running nose.

"Doctor, doctor, I feel like a fly."
   "Would you come down from the ceiling, please?"

What has no legs but walks anyway?
A pair of shoes.

Why did the dog chase his tail?
He wanted to make both ends meet.

How can we be sure that carrots help us see better?
Have you ever seen a rabbit wearing glasses?

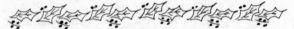

FAIRY SILVER'S FAVOURITE JOKE
Why do bees have sticky hair?
Because they use honeycombs.

How can you tell if an elephant's been sleeping in your bed?
From all the peanut shells.

What is the difference between a flea and an elephant?
An elephant can have fleas but a flea can't have elephants.

NOSEY: Snowball can do bird impressions.
STRIPE: But he's a polar bear!
NOSEY: I know, but he eats worms.

What happens when you cross an elephant and a kangaroo?
You get great big holes all over Australia.

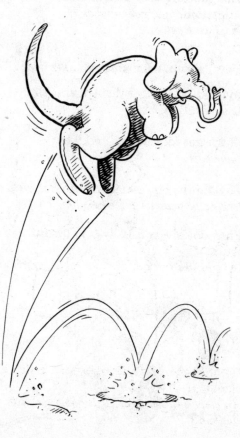

What do you call a very young beetle?
A baby buggy.

FLASH'S FUNNY HA-HA

What do you call two comedians who cure indigestion?
The Two Rennies.

How did Noah steer the Ark at night?
He used floodlights.

What's got four wheels and flies?
A dustcart.

Why did the boy take a ruler to bed with him?
Because he wanted to see how long he slept.

When do drivers usually get punctures in their tyres?
At forks in the road.

MRS SANTA'S CHRISTMAS GIGGLE

SANTA: Are we having Rudolph for Christmas dinner this year?

MRS SANTA: No, we're having turkey as usual.

Why do runners wear shorts?
Because they would be arrested if they didn't.

What is a slug?
A homeless snail.

Which queen of England wore the largest shoes?
The one with the largest feet.

What do you call a bee that has its birthday in May?
A Maybe.

SNOWBALL'S SNIGGERS

Where does a ten tonne polar bear sleep?
Anywhere he wants to.

What did one tonsil say to the other tonsil?
You'd better get dressed up – the doctor's taking us out tonight.

What do you call a man with
a paper bag over his head?
Russell.

What do you call a building
that has a lot of storeys?
A library.

How does Jack Frost
get to work?
By icicle.

Why do bees hum?
*Because they don't know
the words.*

Where do mosquitos
come from?
Stingapore.

What did the bus conductor say to the one-legged passenger?
Hop on!

NOSEY'S CRAZY QUESTION

Why did the robot rub grease all over himself before he went to bed on Christmas Eve?
Because he wanted to wake up oily in the morning.

Why is honey scarce in Manchester?
Because there are no Bs in Manchester.

What kind of cake is best for mopping the floor?
Sponge cake.

Knock, knock.
Who's there?
Buster.
Buster who?
Buster the town centre, please.

SANTA'S CHRISTMAS CHUCKLE

SANTA: I wish you'd pay me a little bit of attention!
STRIPE: I'm paying as little as possible.

What do you call pigs who live together?
Pen friends.

"Waiter, waiter, you've got your thumb on my steak!"

"Yes, sir, I didn't want to drop it on the floor again."

Which monster is the unluckiest in the world?
The Luck Less monster.

RUDOLPH THE REINDEER'S RIDDLE

Why did Rudolph take his red nose apart?
To see what made it run.

What is a cow's favourite TV programme?
Dr Moo.

What is full of holes, yet holds water?
A sponge.

Knock, knock.
Who's there?
Atch.
Atch who?
You've got a terrible cold!

What do parrots eat?
Pollyfilla.

Which famous detective likes taking bubble baths?
Sherlock Foams.

Why shouldn't you go out when it's raining cats and dogs?
You might step in a poodle.

What does a football do when it stops rolling?
It looks round.

What has teeth but can't bite?
A comb.

What do you call an old pig who keeps telling you off?
A boar.

What do tigers sing at Christmas?
"Jungle bells, jungle bells . . . ."

FAIRY SILVER'S FAVOURITE JOKE

Why doesn't Nosey go on holiday abroad?
Because he gets gnomesick.

What happens when you
slip on the ice?
Your bottom gets thaw.

Knock, knock.
Who's there?
Noise.
Noise who?
Noise to see you!

Why do Eskimoes eat candles?
For a little light refreshment.

What sport do horses like best?
Stable tennis.

When is a policeman strong?
When he holds up the traffic.

STRIPE'S SILLY STORY

A teddy bear got a job digging holes on a building site. One day the bell rang for lunch and the bear went with all the other workers to have his sandwiches in the canteen. When we got back he couldn't find his pick anywhere, so he went to report it to the foreman.

"Don't worry," said the foreman. "Didn't you know that today's the day the teddy bears have their picks nicked?"

"Doctor, doctor, my sight seems to be getting very bad."

"I'm afraid this is the Post Office . . . ."

Why don't elephants eat penguins?
Because they can't get the wrappers off.

Why are sardines so stupid?
Because they climb into tins, shut the lid and leave the key on the outside!

FLASH'S FUNNY HA-HA

Flash went to visit one of his friends who was painting the hall. "Why are you wearing so many clothes?" asked Flash.

"Well," said his friend, "it says on the side of the tin, *Put on three coats*, so I have!"

What does a chicken become after it is two months old?
Three months old.

FLASH: I haven't slept for days.
NOSEY: Why not?
FLASH: Because I sleep at night!

What kind of bird steals things?
A robin.

Why do cows wear bells?
Because their horns don't work.

NOSEY'S CRAZY QUESTION

How many presents can Santa fit into an empty sack measuring 2 metres × 2 metres?
One – after that it's not empty any more.

Knock, knock.
Who's there?
Noise.
Noise who?
Noise to see you!

Why are sardines so stupid?
Because they climb into tins, shut the lid and leave the key on the outside!

What do you call a snake with a bowler hat and carrying an umbrella?
A civil serpent.

What is a beetroot?
A potato with high blood pressure?

SNOWBALL'S SNIGGERS

What sort of sheet cannot be folded?
A sheet of ice.

"Waiter, waiter, this coffee tastes like mud!"
  "That's because it's just been ground, sir."

Which football team do squirrels play in?
Nuts Forest.

SANTA'S CHRISTMAS CHUCKLE

How many chimneys does Santa have to climb
down each Christmas?
Stacks.

What happened to the dog who ate nothing but garlic?
His bark was much worse than his bite.

When is a green book not a green book?
When it is read.

What do you call a woman with one leg shorter than the other?
Eileen.

What do you get if you cross a duck and a firework?
A firequacker.

Where do cats keep their cash?
At the Tabby National.

Who tells chicken jokes?
The comedihen.

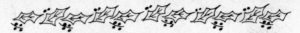

STRIPE'S SILLY STORY

It was a cold, cold winter and the snow lay deep over Scotland. A Red Cross rescue team set out to try to help the residents of one remote village which had been cut off for several days. They were dropped by helicopter, then trudged a longway through snowdrifts to the village, where they dug their way down the high street. Eventually they managed to shovel their way to the front door of one little cottage. They knocked loudly and an old lady opened it a crack.

"Who's that?" she asked.

"It's the Red Cross," said the rescuers.

"It's no good knocking on my door — I gave to charity last year!"

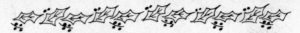

What is a ghost's favourite TV programme?
Horrornation Street.

What lives if you feed it but dies if you water it?
A bonfire.

Why are elephants huge and grey and wrinkly?
*Because if they were small and round and orange
they'd be Smarties.*

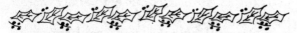

FAIRY SILVER'S FAVOURITE JOKE

Which Christmas pantomime is about a cat in a
chemist's shop?
Puss in Boots.

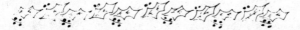

Mrs Santa decided to treat herself to an ice
cream at a cafe. "I'd like a large chocolate fudge
sundae, with banana slices, hot chocolate sauce
and whipped cream."

"Yes, madam," said the waiter. "And a
cherry on the top?"

"Oh no," said Mrs Santa. "I'm on a diet."

Which of Nosey's friends is small, has pointed
ears and solves crimes?
Sherlock Gnomes.

Which animal has the highest intelligence?
The giraffe.

How do you get rid of unwanted varnish?
Take away the R and it vanishes.

What medicine do ants take when they're ill?
Antibiotics.

FLASH'S FUNNY HA-HA

What do you give a nervous elephant?
Trunkquillizers.

How do ghosts like their eggs cooked?
Terrifried!

What kind of wig can hear?
An earwig.

What do you call a nut with a bad memory?
A forget-me-nut.

Where do little fish go each morning?
To plaice school.

MRS SANTA'S CHRISTMAS GIGGLE

Mrs Santa met one of her friends when she was out shopping. "Did you have a nice holiday?" she asked.

"No, it was terrible, it rained every day," said the friend.

"It can't have — you've got a lovely tan," said Mrs Santa.

"That's not a tan, that's rust!"

What's big and hairy and flies faster than the speed of sound?
King Kongcorde.

How many skunks do you need to make a big stink?
Quite a phew!

What do cats rest their heads on at night?
Caterpillars.

What do you call a boy with a rabbit on his head?
Warren.

What do you call a man with a seagull on his head?
Cliff.

SNOWBALL'S SNIGGERS

What animal do you look like when you get into a bath?
A little bear.

Where do gnomes do their shopping?
At British Gnome Stores.

What's the difference between Terry Wogan and the M1?
You can turn off the M1.

Why did J.R. go to court?
To Sue Ellen.

NOSEY'S CRAZY QUESTION

Who invented fire?
Some bright spark.

What do you get if you feed a chicken whisky?
Scotch eggs.

"Waiter, waiter, is there stew on the menu?"
"Yes, sir."
"Well, wipe it off then."

What do you call a man with a bonfire on his head?
Bernard.

Why are rivers rich?
Because they have two banks.

SANTA'S CHRISTMAS CHUCKLE

What does Santa keep even if he gives it away?
A cold.

What are small and furry and go *ee-ee-ee* when you pour milk over them?
Mice Krispies.

What should you say if you meet a monster with three heads?
Hallo, hallo, hallo.

What do you get if you cross a frog and a can of cola?
Croak-a-Cola.

FLASH: I had a terrible dream last night! I dreamt that I was eating very hard crunchy biscuits.
STRIPE: Don't worry, it was only a dream.
FLASH: But when I woke up all the buttons on my pyjamas were missing!

RUDOLPH THE REINDEER'S RIDDLE

"Doctor, doctor, I've just swallowed my guitar!"
"Thank goodness you don't play the piano."

What illness do airline pilots suffer from?
Flu.

What game do four reindeer play in the back of a Mini Metro?
Squash.

What kind of fish is most useful in icy weather?
A skate.

What happened to the man who stole a calendar?
He got twelve months.

What do you get if you cross an elk with a packet of cocoa?
Chocolate mousse.

What do you get if you cross a mouse and a packet of soap powder?
Bubble and squeak.

What do you get if you pour boiling water down a rabbit hole?
Hot cross bunnies.

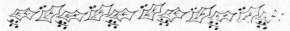

FAIRY SILVER'S FAVOURITE JOKE

SANTA: We went to France last year.
NOSEY: How did you get there?
SANTA: We have a ferry (fairy) at the bottom of our garden.

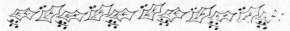

"Doctor, doctor, I've just swallowed a roll of film!"

"You'd better sit down and hope that nothing develops."

What do computers eat with their hamburgers? *Microchips.*

NOSEY: Mrs Santa's being cruel in the kitchen!
STRIPE: What's she doing?
NOSEY: She's whipping the cream and beating the eggs.

What do you call a man who prays in church?
Neil.

STRIPE'S SILLY STORY

The last few drops of the Great Flood were disappearing and Noah was giving the animals a few words of advice before sending them off two by two. "It's all up to you now," he said. "Go forth and multiply. Goodbye, elephants; goodbye, camels; goodbye, rabbits . . . ."

When all the animals had gone Noah went down inside the Ark to pack his own bags and there, hiding, he found two snakes. "Now what are you doing here?" he asked. "Didn't you hear me tell you to go forth and multiply?"

"We can't," hissed the snakes. "We're adders."

Why did the elephant leave the circus?
Because he was sick of working for peanuts.

What did one car say to the other car?
Wheel meet again.

Where can you find the pyramids?
It all depends on where you leave them.

What do you get if you cross a cat with a parrot?

A carrot.

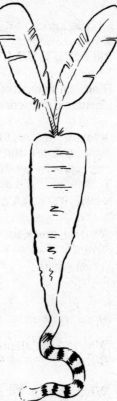

What is yellow and writes?
A ballpoint banana.

Where do bees queue?
At the buzz stop.

What did the big candle say to the little candle?
You're too young to go out tonight.

What could go up a chimney down but not down a chimney up?
An umbrella.

Why did the policeman wear white trousers?
His blue ones were being dry-cleaned.

Knock, knock.
Who's there?
Fiona.
Fiona who?
Fiona had some money I could buy everyone
Christmas presents.

"Doctor, doctor, I keep thinking I'm invisible."
  "I can't see much wrong with you."

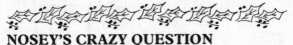

NOSEY'S CRAZY QUESTION

What are green and white and bounce about the
garden?
Spring onions.

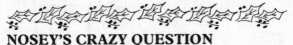

Which football team never meets its opponents
before the match?
Queens Park Strangers.

What's green, hairy and wears sunglasses?
A gooseberry on holiday.

NOSEY: Television will never replace the newspapers.
STRIPE: Why not?
NOSEY: You can't eat fish and chips out of a television.

What has a head but no brain?
A cabbage.

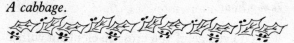

SANTA'S CHRISTMAS CHUCKLE

What's the last thing Santa takes off when he goes to bed on Christmas night?
His feet off the floor.

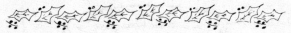

Where do sheep get their hair cut?
The baa-baas.

What do you call a huge monster with cotton wool in his ears?
Anything you like — he can't hear you.

"Doctor, doctor, I keep thinking I'm a carrot."
   "There's no need to get in a stew."

Why did the chickens go to the building site?
Because they wanted to see a man laying bricks.

Which famous spy works under water?
James Pond.

What do you get if you cross an elephant with a goldfish?
Swimming trunks.

What did the mayonnaise say to the fridge?
Please close the door, I'm dressing.

MRS SANTA'S CHRISTMAS GIGGLE

Santa came hurrying in from the Toy Factory one lunchtime. "How long will my sausages be?" he asked.

"About ten centimetres, dear," said Mrs Santa.

"Waiter, waiter, there's a flea in my soup."

"Tell him to hop it, sir."

What's a Laplander?
A clumsy man on a bus.

What do you call a nervous witch?
A twitch.

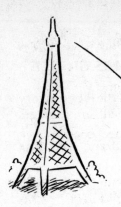

Why shouldn't you jump in the
river that runs through Paris?
Because you would be in Seine.

Which tree is left after a fire?
An ash.

How do you make anti-freeze?
Hide her nightie.

What kind of tea makes you feel good?
Safety.

What's yellow and white and travels at 200 kilometres per hour?
The train-driver's egg sandwich.

RUDOLPH THE REINDEER'S RIDDLE

FLASH: How many legs does Rudolph have?
NOSEY: Four!
FLASH: No, six — he's got forelegs and two back legs.

What do you call a Scottish cloakroom attendant?
Angus McCoat-up.

Why can't an elephant ride a bicycle?
Because he hasn't got a thumb to reach the bell.

What do you call a cow that eats grass?
A lawn-mooer.

Why are Christmas trees
always warm?
Because they're fir trees.

What game do cows play
at parties?
Moo-sical chairs.

What can you get in a cup
but never get out?
A crack.

Nosey's old grandfather came to visit Santa one
day with some jelly and custard stuck in one
ear and some sponge cake behind the other.
   "How are you?" asked Santa.
   "You'll have to speak up," he replied. "I'm a
trifle deaf."

How do sheep keep warm at the North Pole?
By central bleating.

Why did the banana go out with the prune?
Because he couldn't find a date.

AND FINALLY

**WHAT SHOULD EVERYONE IN THE WORLD
GIVE SANTA AND HIS FRIENDS
ON CHRISTMAS MORNING?**

A BIG ROUND OF SANTAPPLAUSE!

Some other Hippo joke books to look out for:

Roland Rat's Rodent Joke Book

0 590 70696 9   £1.25

Roland has selected hundreds of jokes from all the gang including, Fergie's Funny Ha-Ha's, Glenis's Guaranteed Giggles and his very own brill, ace and skill Superstar Collection.

Doggone Dog Joke Book

0 590 70697 7   £1.25

You can't get rid of the dog jokes unleashed in this book until you get to the tail end of Doggone Dog. This collection of canine craziness includes oodles of poodle puns and dozens of doggie giggles.

Grin and Bear It

0 590 70698 5   £1.25

Are you itching to get your paws on an unbearably funny collection of teddy bear jokes, knockout knock knocks and ridiculous riddles?

If you are, then this book's for you.

The Spooktacular Joke Book

0 590 70807 4   £1.25

Do your neighbours disappear at whim? Has your doctor got a bolt through his neck? They don't? He hasn't! You're NOT?! You'd better open up fast — it sounds like you need a dose of the SPOOKTACULAR!

The Tommy Boyd Joke Book

0 590 70639 X   £1.25

Tommy Boyd thinks the Witts are the funniest family in Britain — apart from the Boyds that is! Certainly more jokes are cracked at breakfast than eggs! An ordinary morning with the Witts runs something like this:

" 'Eagh!' gasped father. 'Is this tea or coffee? It tastes like paraffin.'

'It must be tea,' answered Godfrey. 'Mum's coffee tastes like break fluid.' "